The Vietnamese Farm Girl

The Vietnamese Farm Girl
Copyright © 2024 by Robert Domico

Published in the United States of America

Library of Congress Control Number: 2024915245
ISBN   Paperback: 979-8-89091-645-7
ISBN   eBook: 979-8-89091-646-4

All rights reserved. No part of this publication may be reproduced, stored in a retrieval system or transmitted in any way by any means, electronic, mechanical, photocopy, recording or otherwise without the prior permission of the author except as provided by USA copyright law.

The opinions expressed by the author are not necessarily those of ReadersMagnet, LLC.

ReadersMagnet, LLC
10620 Treena Street, Suite 230 | San Diego, California, 92131 USA
1.619. 354. 2643 | www.readersmagnet.com

Book design copyright © 2024 by ReadersMagnet, LLC. All rights reserved.

Cover design by Tifanny Curaza
Interior design by Ched Celiz

The Vietnamese Farm Girl

This is the story of a Vietnamese farm girl who was born out of wedlock, whose father was an American Helicopter Pilot, and whose mother was a young Vietnamese girl in 1964. Her story is an incredible read and you'll find out why.

ROBERT DOMICO

U.S. troops departed Vietnam in March of 1973, and Saigon fell to Communist—no—Vietnamese Forces in April 1975. To some the Vietnam War was a crime. To others, the Vietnam War was a forfeit, a just war needlessly lost by timid policymakers and media.

It was a normal warm day at the Air Force base when a young flyer was writing his parents back home after his break . Afterwards, there was a baseball game, and then, liberty that night, he would go over to the officer's club and play cards, till about 7pm. Then, maybe, stop in the lounge for a drink that night, then call it a night. The young flyer noticed a young Vietnamese girl sitting in the corner, so the young man decided to go over and introduce himself. He walked over very slowly and sat next to this young girl and asked, "What is your name? She replied, "Lilly." He then stayed for a while and talked to the girl, then left to go back to the barracks to go to sleep.

He laid awake for a long time thinking of the girl that he had met. He hoped that he would run into her again. After searching for her for a couple of weeks with no success, he had all but given up on ever seeing her again. He spotted her on the street with a girlfriend and ran up to her saying, "I found you again, nice seeing you. How have you been?" The girl looked up at the tall young man and said "1 am okay." The young Lieutenant asked the girls if they were hungry and would like to get something to eat, they said "Yes that would be nice." The meeting lasted over lunch; the young lieutenant made sure he got the girl's address this time and said he would call her whenever he would get a chance. It hasn't been easy to schedule any kind of meeting with a war going on.

Later that week, he called the girl, and they made arrangements to meet at the officer's club for a day. The young man arrived early, anticipating her arrival and waited for her to come. At about 7:45, the young girl arrived at the officer's club, dressed as he expected. She was even more beautiful than he expected. They sat down casually and dined with anticipated ice from each other. It would be a while before they saw each other again, what with the war going on, and each had their expected roles to perform. The war was long and hard on everybody in that city at that time.

Waking up one morning, the young lieutenant started thinking about the girl again. He couldn't get her out of his mind.

On her way to school one day, when she was seven years old walking down the long path to school, she saw a little girl her own age walking in front of her. It was the first time she had seen this girl, so she called ahead and said, "Are you going to school?"
The girl replied, "Yes, I just moved here from Saigon. "Oh," she said, "My family lives near there, and I live with my grandma on a farm near here." They continued to walk up the path together and she asked the girl what her name was. The girl said, "Lilly, after the Flower."

The girl was shocked, that was her mother's name, which she immediately told the girl. They continued walking down the path. As they spoke, she realized this could

During Her Life with Grandma

One night grandma decided to have a family reunion and get together all the brothers and sisters of Nancy's family. Grandma decided to have a holiday retreat for the whole family, so they decided to rent a villa near Saigon to have a family get together for a week so Nancy could get to know her family, who she was separated from for a long time. The area was very rural, in the middle of nowhere, but it was very expensive, like a large camp ground with a large lake, where the kids could swim and play. It was a weekend and very hot, but it was to be an experience for the girl that she had never seen before. To be together with her whole Family after all these years of being away from them. It was the first Friday night, and they sat around a large campfire, singing old songs from Grandma's repertoire from the old days. They sat around the campfire singing, some dancing and carrying on. Finally, it was time to go sleep, so everyone went into their tents. The night was quiet except for the sound of crickets and an occasional sound of other animals in the distance, howling and carrying on.

The next day everyone was up early, having some special everything soup that Grandma prepared. No one ever figured out exactly what Grandma put into her everything soup, but it tasted good. The next day after breakfast, the whole family went on a long hike along the river side to another rural area deep in the woods, where you could see many deadly reptiles lurking along the path, and many animals swinging from the treetops. They finally arrived in the area where they wanted to go, it was a secluded area, but one of the most beautiful spots in the large forest, with another large lake, with the most beautiful flowers growing all over the place. Nancy always loved flowers, so she spent most of her time picking the flowers and making large bouquets for everyone to enjoy.

The boys were more adventurous, they spent their time chasing animals of all categories, and in some cases playing with them after catching them. Grandma was always cooking and preparing the next meal. The river was loaded with ducks and other game, many kinds of animals, and they caught a lot of shrimp which Grandma prepared for that night's dinner along with some frogs and fish that they caught. Grandmom would chop up a dead banana tree in a big pot to feed the farm animals with. Grandma gave the girl an 18-carat gold and jade Buddha, to wear, but one night she took it off and somebody stole it. Soon after Grandma died when the girl was only 10, she was not able to move back with her mother because her new father was now living out of the area, so she went to live on an army base in Saigon. She pretty much lived by herself, depending on soldiers living in the base with their families to get fed. she would knock on their doors and ask for food, they would give her canned food, opening the cans for Her, and then she would eat, or sometimes they would give her a hoagie or fresh vegetables to eat. She would get a ride to school each day in a jeep and then picked up and bought home, back to the barracks where she lived. She would watch the other kids playing, but they would never let her play with them, because they thought she was odd, so she would play by herself and pretend she was playing with the other children. Finally, after several years in the barracks, her family moved closer to where she was in Can Tho, agar Saigon. And she then moved in back with her mother and new husband, who was the father of all her stepbrothers and sister.

The father opened a little market, where they sold cigarettes, sandwiches, groceries, liquor, soups, etc. Nancy worked in the store for her stepfather for about 5 years, during that time she continued her education going to school and working, until she was old enough to get married. They then arranged a marriage with a medical student, who she then married. A year after they were married, they had a son, Anh. Anh was a bright boy who went to college in the U.S. and graduate with high honors. In 1990, Nancy and her new husband arrived in the U.S.A. They moved to Colorado in with a nice family, Nancy went to work in a grocery store and her husband got a job pumping gas. Nancy started to learn English and immediately started to advance her career, always working one job or another. After several more years working 2 jobs again, she started the task of bringing her family over to America one by one. First, her mother, then her stepfather, then all her stepbrothers and stepsister. By this time, she had moved to Atlantic City, now Jersey, where she made arrangements to rent a house to move her family in. After a couple years, she purchased a house in Atlantic City, before her second son was born. She put her sons into a Catholic school in Atlantic City called Our Lady of the Sea, where they attended school and went to church there also. She continued working 1.5 jobs for years, before she landed the job of her dreams at the new Borgata that was about to open. Presently, she is still there after 14 years since its opening late 2003 as a supervisor and dealer. She still makes grandma's soup, recently she purchased several large whole lobsters. Everyone thought that they were going to have drawn butter and lobster but instead she served the lobster in soup the old-fashioned way.

documents. The letters describe common occurrences of civilian killings during occupation. Pacific Army policy also stressed very high body counts and this resulted in dead civilians being marked as combatants. Alluding to indiscriminate killings described as unavoidable, the commander of the 9th, Major General Julian Ewell, in September 1969, submitted a confidential report to Westmoreland and generals describing the countryside in some areas of Vietnam as resembling the battlefields of Verona.

In July 1969, the Office of Provost Marshal General of the Army began to examine the evidence. Co-General Peers inquiry regarded possible criminal charges. Eventually, Calley was charged with premeditated murder in September 1969, and 25 other officers and enlisted men were later charged crimes.

Court Martial

On November 17, 1970, a court-martial in the United States charged 14 officers, including Major Genaral Koster, the American Division's commanding officer, with suppressing information related to the in the charges were later dropped. Brigade commander Colonel Henderson was the only high-ranking officer who stood trial on charges relating to the cover-up of the My Lai massacre; he was acquitted 17, 1971.[90]

During the four-month-long trial, Lieutenant Calley consistently claimed that he was following orders from commanding officer, Captain Medina. Despite that, he was convicted and sentenced to life in prison in 1971, after being found guilty of premeditated murder of not fewer than twenty people. Two days after, one Richard Nixon made the controversial decision to have Calley released from armed custody at Fort Georgia and put under house arrest pending appeal of his sentence. Calley's conviction was upheld at the Court of Military Review in 1973 and by the U.S. Court of Military Appeals in 1974.[91] In August, the sentence was reduced by the Convening Authority from life to twenty years. Calley would spend one-and-a-half years under house arrest at Fort Benning, including three months in a disciplinary barracks in Leavenworth, Kansas. In September 1974, he was paroled by the Secretary of the Army Howard C

In a separate trial, Captain Medina denied giving the orders that led to the massacre, and was acquitted of all charges, effectively negating the prosecution's theory of "command responsibility", now referred to as "standard". Several months after his acquittal, however, Medina admitted that he had suppressed evidence and lied to Colonel Henderson about the number of civilian deaths. [93] Captain Kotouc, an intelligence officer from the 11th Brigade, was also court-martialed and found not guilty. Major General Koster was demoted to general and lost his position as the Superintendent of West Point. His deputy, Brigadier General Yc letter of censure. Both were stripped of Distinguished Service Medals which had been awarded for Vietnam.[94]

Most of the enlisted men who were involved in the events at My Lai had already left military service. Out of the 26 men initially charged, Lieutenant Calley was the only one convicted.

Some have argued that the outcome of the My Lai courts-martial failed to uphold the laws of war e

she was with her girl friend, she was told if you want to meet someone nice that you should get into dancing. I'll never forget that first night I ever saw her, she was with her girl friend and I was with another girl that I had met a few weeks before. We were all taking turns dancing with each other. It's called a mixer. The ladies line up on one side of the room and the gentlemen also in line, dance with the girl who is ever next in line. We were doing a waltz mixer as I recall. We met that night. I liked her right away, here was this beautiful, very cute Vietnamese girl and me. It was a match made in Heaven.
We started dating and the rest is history. A couple years after we met, we decided to do some traveling. First, I took her to London and then to Paris. She had only been to Vietnam, and then to America. She had never really traveled much in her life. After,

we were together for 10 years, and I took her back to Vietnam where she hadn't been for many years. Last year, Nancy, without any formal education, was in the top 40% income bracket in the United States.

With the war coming to an end, it was hard for everybody to identify who they really were.
Where a **Vietnased to.mesa** people buy were sorted out by their beliefs, some were communists, and others were trapped in the belief that they were victims of an unnecessary war. The farm girl was taken right from the hospital as an infant to the farm and didn't know anything else but Grandma in her life. When Grandma died, she was left in a state of shock, she didn't know what to do anymore. She was forced to go back with her biological mother, who didn't have a lot of time for her. By now she had her own family and wasn't happy taking her daughter back. The girl was forced when she left the farm, which was all she ever knew and cared about in her life. The girl, after that, was sent to live with an American soldier's family in Saigon where she attended school and lived on canned rations and not too much homemade food that she was used to from living her whole life with Grandma.

It was a hard life for grandma and the girl didn't know if the soldiers would take what you gave them to eat and leave, or if they would kill you. Carrying around guns and having vengeance in their hearts. After Grandma died, the girl had mixed emotions about the way she felt, not being able to forget about grandma and then coping with a new kind of life, a life that she had never experienced before.

Probably the one thing that kept her alive and still helped her was that she was young and unknowing about the ways of the world. The girl was raised in the best of care, she was in a war that she didn't want, that nobody wanted, but she put up with it because she had no choice. She was made to live in that environment weather she like it or not. The war went on and the then finally ended, and she was in the middle of it and couldn't do anything about it.

She dreaded going back to her mother who had abandoned her when she was a baby. And then, moving back in with her newfound brothers and sister would be more than she would be able to bear. After living in an American Army camp, that was bad enough, so finally she moved back with her family.
Grandma was gone and it seemed like the world was closing in on her, first the war and then this. She was lucky in a way, because most of the Vietnamese children were abandoned by their parents. At least she had grandma, who protected her from everything you could imagine. Most of the children grew up as leftovers.

In a war, most never knew their fathers, many were abandoned by their mothers at the gates of institutions, not knowing who their fathers where. Some had round blue eyes and some had dark skin if their fathers where African Americans. They Iived around parks and on the streets, President Gerald Ford planned to evacuate 2000 children from Saigon and take them to the U.S. but the plane crashed in the rice paddies near Saigon, with 144 aboard. The evacuation lasted another 3 weeks after that.

Saigon was a city in reins after the war, what was once a beautiful city had become a desolate area, The beautiful, tree lined city was elegant, with its international look, with beautiful European people standing around and inside the restaurants and taverns.

As the war was coming to an end and the bullets stopped flying around, it seemed quieter now with bombs exploding and no guns going off, no hand grenades going off. With grandma gone, the girl moved back to Saigon with her mother for a while and then, with her father working away most of the time, she moved in with an American soldier's family at age 9 till she was 12. She immediately found friends and, continuing her schooling, she worked in her mother's convenience store which sold liquor, groceries, and a variety of sandwiches, that's where she got her first experience in making and waitressing. The girl never had a chance to get a good education. The girl was very healthy and strong, when she dressed up, she looked like a tomboy in lace. She was a very attractive young lass.

Her biological parents, when she got older, arranged a marriage for her at 19 which was the custom in those days. They arranged a marriage with a young medical student who later became a doctor. When she was 20, she had her first son because her father was an American Soldier. It was easy for her to gain passage to the United States. The girl and her new husband moved to the USA. Several years after she got pregnant again and had another son. Because her husband was not educated in the U.S. he was never certified in the medical field in the U.S. and got a job pumping gas. The girl, not being good at English got a job as a maid in an Atlantic City Hotel. And then several waitress jobs after, she went to dealer's school for the casinos in Atlantic City and started dealing cards.

Nancy has her little quirks, like when you're driving and you are on the outside lane, she worries that person coming towards you will have a heart attack and come over and cause a head-on collision with you. From living with her for years I have learned all about her little fears. She has little pains in her shoulders and back and wrist from dealing cards for so many years . She has a strong desire to open a liquor store here in the United States and get away from the pain of dealing cards for so many years, of people blowing smoke in her face and coughing in her face, she just wants to be her own boss now, since her kids are grown and can take care of herself now. We have a modest, 3-bedroom two bath colonial house about 30 miles from Atlantic City. She stays in town 5 days when she is working and comes home for 2 days a week. We are now planning a cruise to the Mediterranean, where we fly over to Barcelona, Spain, and get on a cruise ship and cruise to 10 counties and wind up in London, England, and then take off for home back to Philadelphia, PA, and then drive home from there. This is an experience that we have been talking about for a long time.

The farm had two turkeys that would keet strangers from entering the front gate, they would peck at the stranger who would come to the gate, denying them entrance into the yard by pecking at them as they tried to enter the premises. If they were fortunate enough to get in, they would continue to peck at them during their entire stay, they were the guard dogs for the farm. During the war, their were many soldiers from all sides that would visit the farm at different times. Maybe they wanted something to eat or to purchase food or to just hang out for a spell. None would ever be denied entrance by grandma, who treated everyone the same. After all, they were just soldiers fighting for whatever cause. The solders would purchase items from grandma, to eat or for other needs that they may have and whatever they wanted, they could buy, and grandma would always make her rice wine that she would sell to the solders.

It was always dangerous during the war. There would be bullets flying around, you would have to keep your head low most of the time. Grandma would go down to the river to catch fish or paddle up to the market to sell items or purchase items for her own use. The farmgirl would always have mud on her face, so she wouldn't be attractive to the solders while she was growing up. After the war things started to lighten, but then in 1975 the communists took over the county, and everything changed again. When Grandma died, the girl was made to move in with her mother in Saigon. Her mother's family had a deli and liquor store, where you could buy any food or beverage. The girl worked in the store after school, until she was about 17. Then, she entered into an arranged marriage with her soon to be husband. The girl's husband was in medical school leaning to be a Doctor. realizing it was on somebody else's property where she found the beautiful flowers. The neighbor came by to complain to grandma that her granddaughter had taken her flowers, but grandma agreed to compensate her for her loss by giving her something in return. Grandma was a good negotiator, so she very quickly solved the problem. There were many animals on the farm, which most of the time considered were pets. Such was the case with the male and female turkeys, who actually guarded the gate of the farm, the farm had boards pile on top of each other creating a fence around the prop with an opening in from of the farm house, where the turkeys would push away oncoming visitors and would make noise and actually push away potential invaders to the property, especially if you were near their chicks. Grandma would always sell her rice wine and eggs from chickens and duck eggs she would gather along the banks of the river. She also grew many vegetables that she would sell to soldiers from all sides of the war. Americans, North and South Vietnamese soldiers and civilians, she took the money and transferred it into gold and buried it in the ground on the farm. It was a good thing that the girl had her grandma to teach her little tricks like how to catch shrimp in a casting net and how to paddle a ci using the side-to-side method and the J stroke. Growing up in such an environment must have been very trying for the young girl, especially with the war going on, all around. One night, grandma got sick and there was no one around. The young girl did not know what to do, so she ran to the nearby telephone which was 1.5 miles away and called her mother in Saigon, and her mother and a friend came running. The man that her mother brought with her to help with her mother put Grandma on his back and ran through the mud to the nearest medical establishment to help Grandma, but by time he got to the medical establishment, Grandma had passed away.

The farm girl would pick up duck eggs along the river side to bring home for her and grandma to Eat. Grandma would take the girl to the river with her and catch catfish. Grandma would let the girl stay in the canoe tied up to a tree. The canoe was made out of boards, and then a thick glue was put on the outside and then they would let it dry out for six months to get the glue hard. When Grandma would go along the shallow water near the edge of the river and on her hands and knees and put her head under the water and look for catfish, when she saw the catfish under the water in the catfish hole on the bottom, she would reach down with both hands, one on each side of the fish, down in the hole and grasp the fish. One hand would be on either side and she would bring it up, being careful not to cut her hands on the sharp fins on the back and head of the fish. After she got the fish home, she would filet the fish and put salt and pepper on it and dry it out in the sun for several weeks, being careful to take it in every night so that big birds wouldn't come and eat the fish. When she finally dried out the catfish, she would hang them in the kitchen, so if they didn't have fresh fish to eat that night, her and the girl would eat the dried fish with white rice that night for dinner. Each morning grandma would go down to the river and cast a net out to catch shrimp, then she would take the shrimp home and put it on top of the charcoaled wood that she had made earlier, with more wood to heat the charcoal so that the shrimp would have just the right taste. frequent and the nation would be overrun by Communists backed soldiers. The area around the farm became much quieter with no more American soldiers coming around anymore, grandma decided to reduce the risk of anyone coming to the farm and maybe asking for more food and rice wine now that the communists were in charge of the country and thought they had more power over people. She built a more secure fence around the farm, making entry more difficult for the soldiers so that trespassing wouldn't be so easily.

couple of years older, she could maybe protect her. As they continued to walk, the young girl asked her new friend, "What do you like to do?" The girl replied, "I play the flute." The girl replied, "Oh that's nice, I can sing a little." The young girl realized that maybe now she would have someone to play with, someone her own age. Whenever she would try to play with other kids, she was always an outcast, the other kids thought she was odd, for some reason.
When they got to school, they sat next to each other. After school, they walked home together, talking and carrying on. She thought about inviting the girl to meet Grandma and maybe play together

on the weekend. The girl had other plans that weekend, she was visiting her cousin, but

be a new friend for her, someone to play with, and she was a

When a girl is born out of wedlock, it was considered an outrageous thing in Vietnam, so the mother of the farm girl was embarrassed to tell anyone about her baby girl. So, grandma said, "Just don't tell anyone you have that daughter. I will raise the young girl for you, and no one needs to know ever." When the girl's mother met another man when the girl was about 5 years old, she didn't tell him until they were together for a few years that she had another child, but her new husband loved her enough that he didn't care anyway.

Down the road was the farmgirl, her name was Nancy. She had a sister and 3 brothers, so the girl was the eldest in her family. When she grew older, about 20, she was put into an arranged marriage, which was somewhat customary in Vietnam in some cases. The girl was introduced to a young man who was a medical student in Vietnam, and they had a very large wedding of about 250 people. Because the girl had an American father, she and her husband were allowed to move to the United States. They were put with family in Colorado. The girl had a hard time, not speaking any English made getting a job difficult, and her husband, not having any experience in the medical profession, had to go to work pumping gas. So finally, they wound up moving to Atlantic City New Jersey, where gambling had come in just a few years before.

Nancy's first job was as a bus girl in one of the larger restaurants in Atlantic City. She liked the job, there were nice people coming into the restaurant and her co-workers were good to her, treating her like one of them. After a while, she became a cook and then a waitress, and then one day she decided to go to dealer's school to deal cards in one of the local casinos. She finished school and got a job at the Claridge Casino as a croupier (a dealer of cards in a gambling game.) She stayed at the Claridge for 7 years, then the Resorts International for two years and then two years at Trump Marina Casino. This started a long career of dealing cards that would take her into the job she presently has now, 30 years later. After Nancy arrived in the United States, she felt a need to try to help her family still in Vietnam by first sending them money and then doing everything in her power to try to bring them over here into the United States, one by one. Her husband still not pursuing his medical career and still pumping gas for a living, very quickly went through the gold that his family had given him when he came to the United States and entered into carefree life of gambling and not at all conducting himself as a husband and now father of two beautiful boys. Nancy Ignored his flamboyant life and concentrated on working hard, most of the time keeping two jobs to keep her sons in school and pay all the bills. Her husband continued his wild lifestyle and eventually found himself out on the street with no wife and no kids. She filed for divorce, finally letting him go. Nancy's golden dream was having her entire family over to the United States, and after years of effort, years of working two jobs and dealing with passports and all the red tape to make the dream a reality, she finally succeeded in getting her entire family to the United States, getting them here and getting them all jobs in Atlantic City. After working at the Claridge Casino in Atlantic City for a couple of years, Nancy felt it was time to move on with her career, so she left there and when to work for the Tropicana Casino in Atlantic City where she learned to deal all the Casino Games. Nancy worked in 5 different casino's before she found her final home at the Borgata Casino in Atlantic City. She was one of the first people hired in the very large and beautiful Casino in Atlantic City. After she went to Borgata, she moved up very quickly from dealer, to pit boss, and then supervisor.

her emotions and the lovely way she presented herself. After several more dates, they found they had an afternoon with nothing to do, so they both decided to register in a hotel and sleep together. He had hinted around for days to do so. After the hotel room they were inseparable, they had to be with each other almost every day. He would leave and maybe go to Bangkok to pick up troops that were coming into Vietnam for the first time, as his job was as a pilot for incoming troops, to fly the troops in from Bangkok Thailand into Saigon to fight in the war for the south. The young girl at that point had gotten pregnant with a baby girl, who was to become the Vietnamese Farm Girl. Soon after the young girl got pregnant, the Young Lieutenant was killed when his plane full of troops was shot down while taking troops into Vietnam.

When the baby was born, because the young girl had a baby out of wedlock, which is forbidden in Vietnam, the baby, when it was old enough to leave its mother, moved out to the country with her grandma. The grandmother lived out in the Vietnamese countryside on farm. It was a quiet place, way out of the way, but still the war was going on. Each night the baby's grandma would put the girl in a hammock in the small house and put and little net around her so the mosquitos didn't bite her. There were many animals on the farm. Chicken, goats, horses, cows, ducks, and pigs.

Each day the grand would get up early and feed all the animals and then go out to the field and attend the vegetables of many varieties.

The plants would literally grow by themselves as it rained every day. The chickens would lay eggs, and Grandma would sell them to people who would come to the farm to buy them. The snakes in the area would come in and wrap themselves around the chickens, choke them, and eat them. Grandma had a long stick about 10 feet long, she would push the snakes away from the chickens to make them leave. She would wake up in the middle of the night, when she heard the chickens making a lot of noise, then go out and push the snakes away from the chickens. If the snake bit the chicken and injected poison inside, then Grandma would bury the chicken. It wasn't safe to eat with the snake's poison inside.

There were many soldiers who would come by from both sides of the war, stopping at grandma's farm to get food and vegetables and meat, and grandma made rice wine and sold it to the soldiers who would stop and buy wine and vegetables and meat from grandma. During the war the bugs were flying by about 3.5 feet off the ground, so you had to keep your head down or crawl on the ground to get around. Grandma would give the old rice from the wine making process and they would walk around like they were drunk from the rice.

The Vietnam horses were smaller than regular horses, such as American horses or Arabian horse, almost the size of a pony. There were many other animals on the farm such as cows, ducks, pigs, cats, dogs, etc. Grandma would reach up with a long stick with a hook knife on the end and cut the coconuts to get them down from the tree and also cotton to stuff the pillows with for sleeping. She would also follow the ducks around from the river and get their eggs to eat. In the morning, a couple times a week, grandma would go down to the river and get in her canoe and paddle up the river to watch the tides to make sure the tide was going her way. She would go on into the town and sell

The Vietnamese Farm Girl

During her life, the young girl was moved from place to place. When grandma died, she was made to move back with her mother to Saigon, but her mother now had, at this point, several more children. Her mother's new husband (her stepfather) worked as a detective for the government and moved around a lot, making it more difficult for her to move in with him. She was put with a military family, in a camp with American soldiers and their families as a foster child from age 8 to age 12. Then, she moved back with her stepfather and mother, to Vinh Long, Vietnam, with her brothers and sister. Minht, boy, Thuy, girl, and Hal, boy. The girl was never happy in Vietnam. She was born 6 years before the war started, then made to live with her grandmother until she was 8, so most of her friends were killed or maimed. When she moved back with her mother, she worked in her mother's store, which sold sandwiches, can goods, and liquor. Her stepfather was a detective who was made to travel a lot to different areas of Vietnam. The girl lived with her parents until she was old enough to get married, and then had a wedding arranged when she was 19 with the medical student. They moved to the United States after 5 years. Because her biological father was American, she got to move to the United States with her husband.

she said the following weekend she was open. On the following weekend, the girl showed up at grandma's with her older brother and sister, which was fine with her. They all frolicked in the back of the house all day on Saturday. The young girl had found a new friend and wouldn't be bored anymore. When grandma always asked the young girl what she was doing, she would always say, "I'm bored!" and Grandma would always say, "Go out and feed the chickens.", and the girl would say, "That's your job grandma!", then Grandma would always say, "Then stay there and be more bored."

Down the road there was a farmgirl, her name was Phuong until she arrived in the United States, then she changed her name to Nancy. When she arrived in the United States her son Anh was only 9 years old, and the girl needed an American name, so her son who was only 9 years old at the time, said there is a girl in school who shares her lunch box with me, named Nancy, and she treats him nice. I like that name, so I took the name of Nancy. From that day forward, she told everybody my son gave me the name Nancy and they laugh at me, said the girl.

During the war, it was hard living with bullets flying around 18 inches off the ground. You could literally raise your hands up and get a manicure. The girl, most of her life because she was a young female, had to cover her face in mud so she wouldn't be attractive to the passing soldiers in the area. Grandma kept a watchful eye, always protecting her, but towards the end of the war it was hard to hide her beauty. Grandma always sold something or another to the soldiers. Rice wine, vegetables, other food items that she would mostly manufacture, all of which she would get paid for and then trade the money for gold. To grandma there wasn't anything more valuable than gold, of course grandma died unexpectedly in the middle of the night, and she never told anyone where the gold was buried.

When the family all moved back to the U.S. they left Grandma's property in the hands of a relative, who sold off most of Grandma's land, because if you left Vietnam you could not own anything there you just had to leave everything, so the farmgirl's mother left everything in the care of an aunt and the aunt sold everything off, never compensating the girl's mother for anything. There were sad times and many losses that the poor people of Vietnam had to give up and leave behind because of a bad government situation there. The Vietnamese war was started by President John F. Kennedy when he bought experienced military trainers in aide and trained the South Vietnamese soldiers to fight the North Vietnamese soldiers backed by the Communists. Over two million Vietnamese people were killed, and 58,000 American soldiers died in the Vietnam War. President Richard Nixon ended the long unnecessary war, pulling the American troops out the war. The war lasted through the terms of four United States presidents. Afterwards, with all that fighting the Communist party took over Vietnam in 1975 anyway. If you go there now you will see Russian flags on every corner.

The Vietnamese Farm Girl

Prelude to the book, Bob Domico, the author, writes in a manner that makes you feel that you are there in Vietnam in the 1970s, going through the trials and tribulations of the characters in the story who actually lived these events. He explains each detail with extreme clarity, describing each incident with exact detail, so the reader can feel the impact of the situations.

The war started in 1962 and ended in 1967. President Kennedy sent trainers over to Vietnam to train the south Vietnam solders to teach them how to defend themselves for they were inexperienced fighters. When the girl was 7 or 8 years old, the girl had beautiful, long black hair. In order for the girl not to seem unattractive to the solders, grandma used to take the burnt marks off the bottom of the pot and rub it into the girl's hair along with mud and cut it in 5 or 6 places, so that she wouldn't be attractive to the soldiers who visited the farm. Doing the war the helicopters would fly overhead and warn the people that they would be fighting the next day and to take shelter. The girl and grandma would a find hole that people would defecate in, which had two boards on top to seat on to do your business and a pot in the bottom to catch everything in. Bright and early in the morning Grandma would take everything out of the hole and crawl down in the hole with the girl, so that they would be low enough to be 18 inches below the flying bullets overhead.

Grandma would say to the girl, "If you want to live, keep your head down." One time when they went to the hole, there was a viper inside, so grandma had to take a long stick to get the snake out before they crawled inside. So, grandma and the girl laid inside the hole till the fighting stopped. Grandma and the girl would stay down 18 inches under the flying bullets overhead. Grandma and the girl would stay in the hole on an average of After the bullets stopped being fired overhead, grandma and the girl would go back to the farm and soldiers from both sides would stop and ask questions of them to get information about the war. The girl was asked "Who comes into your house?" She was always told by Grandma not to say anything to the soldiers to just act stupid. The soldiers would ask who was the girl's mother and they would offer the young girl candy and cookies, but the girl never answered. When the soldiers would ask where the girl's mother was, grandma would answer the girl's mother is working as a maid in Saigon. The girl's mother would come home to the farms every couple of months and bring gold to grandma. Grandma would put salt and rice over top of the gold, when Grandma died the secret of where the gold was buried, never told to the girl's mother.

Many times, grandma would make her soup. The girl would say, "What kind of soup is it?" Grandma would say, "Everything soup." The girl would say, "What is in it?" Grandma would say, "Everything is in it." The girl would say, "I don't want to eat it if it doesn't have a name." Grandma would say, "You don't have to." The the girl would look around the house and see what else there was to eat, and didn't find anything but a banana and an apple. So, this would go on all the time, then finally the girl would try the soup and would always say it was good. By this time, she was hungry. The girl would have a small bowl, and after that she said it was good, and asked if she could have another bowl. Afterwards, the girl would say it was good the same day she would wash clothes, Grandma would ask the girl to fold the clothes and put them away. The girl would say, "I don't have to fold the clothes, I live here with you. I don't have to fold the clothes." Grandma would say, "Oh yes, then I'll give you back to your mother and you can live with her. The girl said, "I don't want to move back in with my mother, I want to stay here with you Grandma." Grandma would say, "If you want to stay here you have to fold the clothes and put them away for me." The girl would give in and fold the cloths for Grandma. The girl said, "I don't want to fold the clothes, Grandma said you to fold the cloths, you live here you have to help me." The girl said, "No, I belong to you, I don't work for you. Grandma said I can't wait for your mother to come; I will give you back to her." The girl said, "I don't belong to you, I don't want to go back with my mom." The girl's mother gave birth to her out of wedlock, so they never spoke about where she came from. When her mother would come to visit she call her aunt (Vu) (Nuoi)

At the beginning of the war and during the war, Grandma would wake up every morning and gather the burned bottom of pots and rub it into the farm girl's long hair to distract any and all military personnel from looking at her. She was only a child, but she had beautiful long hair. Every night the helicopters would fly over the farm and on a loudspeaker would announce that tomorrow the fighting would begin again. The next morning, Grandma and the girl would find a hole to climb into and stay below 18 inches off the ground from where the bullets were flying overhead. It was probably the most dangerous place you could have been, because the communist controlled North Vietnamese had already killed 4000 South Vietnamese Citizens. They killed men, old men, women, children, and animals in many of the countryside villages for no reason, so life was cheap there.

In 1962, with threat of the communist controlled North Vietnam planning to attack south Vietnam, president Kennedy sent instructors to teach the south Vietnamese to fight when the war started. The war was a long hard battle between the south Vietnamese and the North Vietnamese, also called the Viet Cong. Each night before a day of fighting the Helicopters would fly overhead and announce over loud speakers that the fighting would start the next morning to for the people who lived on the ground to take cover in the morning. The farm girl and her Grandma would find a hole in the ground, usually there were holes in the ground where people would defecate in, which was a hole in the ground with two boards to sit on and do your business in. There would be a pot in the bottom to catch everything in. Grandma would remove the pot and have her and the girl lay in the space in the bottom, which would put them about 18 inches under the flying bullets overhead. One time, when Grandma removed the pot, there was a snake in the hole. Grandma had to take a long stick and remove the pit viper before they could go inside. In the hole, Grandma and the girl would be at least 18 inches under the bullets flying overhead.

Grandma would tell the girl if she wanted to live, she must stay down. Every day, soldiers from both sides would visit the farm and grandma did her best to prepare whatever food she had to feed them. Sometimes she would kill a chicken and cook it for them, and sometimes just make them eggs or whatever. As the girl grew a little older, Grandma would, rub her hand on the bottom of a pot that she had cooked in to rub on the girl's face so that she would look less attractive to the soldiers. she would cut her hair and rub the bottom of the pots on her face so she would smell bad and look bad, after all, it was war time, and anything goes. The soldiers would ask Grandma and the girls who were there last, and when they were there and if they knew where they were going. The American soldiers would offer candy to get information, and the Vietcong would threaten the grandma and the farmgirl. They would ask who was coming in the house and asking questions. Grandma would tell the girl to say no one came and asked anything. It was a life of horror for the little girl for years until the war ended.

"Did they survive?': children of the Vietnam war, 50 years on | Global | The Guardian he would lie awake at night, terrorized by the smells and sounds of battle. Returning to Vietnam with Larry and Rod for the first time since he left a burning Saigon 45 years ago has helped him, he says, "To see Vietnam as a country and as a society, rather than only as a war."

Minh is now a cockfighter, who lives in Vung Tau with his wife and children, Photograph: Reed Young

Rod, now 70, agrees. "It gave me the sense of finishing the circle."

Using old army maps and GPS satellite images, Larry, Del, and Rod were able to pinpoint exactly where Jeff had been killed, and they buried a box of mementoes and medals there.

"There was so much laughter and so many tears." says Larry upon meeting the Chon Thanh villagers and his time in Vietnam. "It was the most incredible experience of my life."

Additional reporting by Ngoc Nguyen Thanh.

Since you're here…

…we have a small favour to ask. More people are reading the Guardian than ever, but advertising revenues across the media are falling fast. And unlike many news organisations, we haven't put up a paywall—we want to keep our journalism as open as we can. So you can see why we need to ask for your help. The Guardian's independent, investigative journalism takes a lot of time, money, and hard work to produce. But we do it because we believe our perspective matters—because it might well be your perspective, too.

I appreciate there not being a paywall: it is more democratic for the media to be available for all and not a commodity to be purchased by a few. I'm happy to make a contribution so others with less means still have access to information. Thomasine F-R.

If everyone who reads our reporting, who likes it, helps to support it, our future would be much more secure.

Become a supporter
Make a contribution
Topics
- Vietnam
- Asia Pacific

The Vietnamese Farm Girl

45. Angers, Trent. *The Forgotten Hero of My Lai: The Hugh Thompson Story, Revised Edition.* Lafayette, I Acadian House, pp.59-78. Print.
46. Angers, Trent. *The Forgotten Hero of My Lai: The Hugh Thompson Story, Revised Edition.* Lafayette, I Acadian House, pp.74. Print.
47. Angers, Trent. *The Forgotten Hero of My Lai: The Hugh Thompson Story, Revised Edition.* Lafayette, I Acadian House, pp.77. Print.
48. "Hugh Thompson". *The Times.* London. January 11, 2006. Retrieved May 2, 2010.
49. Angers, Trent. *The Forgotten Hero of My Lai: The Hugh Thompson Story, Revised Edition.* Lafayette, I Acadian House, pp.79. Print.
50. Angers, Trent. *The Forgotten Hero of My Lai: The Hugh Thompson Story, Revised Edition.* Lafayette, I Acadian House, pp.80. Print.
51. Bock, Paula. The Choices Made: Lessons from My Lai on Drawing the Line. (http://scattletimes.com/p10/cover.html) Archived (https://web.archive.org/web/20141008060011/http://seattletimes.com/pacific ver.html) October 8, 2014, at the Wayback Machine. *The Seattle Time,* March 10, 2002.
52. Angers, Trent. *The Forgotten Hero of My Lai: The Hugh Thompson Story, Revised Edition.* Lafayette, I Acadian House, pp.86. Print.
53. The Heroes of My Lai: Hugh Thompson' Story (http://law2.umkc.edu/faculty/projects/ftrials/mylai/MN) Thompson's own account during the conference on My Lai at Tulane University in New Orleans, December 1994.

54. Clenn Urban Andreotta (http://thewall-usa.com/info.asp?recid=1110) Names on the Wall, The Vietnam Memorial.
55. Robert Fowler (August 4, 2010). "Glenn Urban Andreotta". Find A Grave. Retrieved April 19, 2011.
56. Bilton, M., & Sim, K. (1992). *Four hours of My Lai: The Hugh Thompson Story*. LA Acadian House. | ISBN 978-0-925417-33-6.
57. Rhoda Koenig (1992). "Books: Enemies of the People". *New York Magazine*. New York Media, LLC.: ISSN 0028-7369. Retrieved April 19, 2011.
58. Adam Jones (2010). Genocide: A Comprehensive Introduction. Taylor & Francis. p. 408. ISBN 978-0-
59. Johnson, Claudia D., & Vernon Elso Johnson (2003). *Understanding the Odyssey: a student casebook. and historic documents.* Westport, CT: Greenwood Publishing Group. p. 206. ISBN 978-0-313-30881-
60. "Heroes of My Lai honored" (http://news.bbc.co.uk/1/hi/special_report/1998/03/98/mylai/62924.stm) BBC News.
61. John Zutz (1998). "My Lai". *The Veteran*. Vietnam Veterans Against the War. **28** (1). Retrieved April
62. "Hugh Thompson: Helicopter pilot who intervened to save lives during the U.S. Army massacre of Vie at My Lai". The Times. January 11, 2006. Retrieved April 19, 2011.
63. "Moral Courage In Combat: The My Lai Story" (PDF). USNA Lecture. 2003.
64. Bilton, Michael, and Kevin Sim. *Four Hours in My Lai*. New York: Viking, 1992.
65. Medina said to have "encouraged" murder (https://news.google.com/newspapers?id=MGxkAAAAIBA

AAIBAJ&pg=2313,475102&dq=-my+lai+medina+knock+off+the+killing&hl=en). *The Calgary Herald.* 1971.
66. The Omissions and Commissions of Colonel Oran K. Henderson (http://www.law.umkc.edu/faculty/pr i/Henderson.html). An extract from the official U.S. Army *Peers Report* into My Lai Massacre. University Kansas City Law school website.
67. Angers (1999), pp. 219-220.
68. Bourke, Joanna. An Intimate History of Killing: Face-to-Face Killing in Twentieth-Century Warfare. (le.com/books?id=J_kMuQVXFkgC&pg=PA417&dq-Four+Hours+in+My+Lai:+A+War+Crime+and+sa-X&ei-ZLMrUvi40tWg4APWvIGwCg&ved-0CDEQ6AEwBA#/v=onepage&q=%20My%20 New York, NY: Basic Books, 1999.
69. Westmoreland, William C. *A Soldier Reports.* Garden City, N. Y.: Doubleday, 1976, p. 378.
75. "Interview on CNN's Larry King Live with Secretary Colin L. Powell". May 4, 2004. Archived from t1 2006-03-09. Retrieved March 16, 2006.
76. "Text of Ron Ridenhour's 1969 letter". Law.umkc.edu. 1969-03-29. Retrieved 2012-07-21.
77. "The Heroes of My Lai". Law.umke.edu. December 1994. Retrieved 2012-07-21.
78. The Men Talked of the Killing (https://news.google.com/newspapers?id-FEUyAAAAIBAJ&sjid=2bU=979,32153&dq-michael+terry+my+lai&hl-en). *The Palm Beach Post*, June, 1970.
79. The Heroes of My Lai: Ron Ridenhour's Story (http://law2.umkc.edu/faculty/projects/ftrials/mylai/MyN) Ridenhour's

own account during the conference on My Lai at Tulane University in New Orleans, L December 1994.
80. "Mo Udall, The Education of a Congressman". Udall.gov. Retrieved 2011-06-18.
81. Brooke, Edward William (2007). *Bridging the Divide: My Life.* Rutgers University Press. p. 166. ISBN
82. Friday, Dec. 05, 1969 (1969-12-05). "The Press: Miscue on the Massacre", Time.com. Retrieved 2011-
83. Oliver, Kendrick (2006). *The My Lai Massacre in American History and Memory.* Manchester: Manch Press. p. 48. ISBN 0719068916.
84. Linder, Douglas (1999). "Biography of General William R. Peers". Law.umke.edu. Retrieved 2011-06-
85. 'Ltc Frank Akeley Barker". Thewall-usa.com. 1967-11-26. Retrieved 2011-06-18.
86. Schell, Jonathan. *The Military Half: An Account of Destruction in Quang Ngai and Quang Tin.* New
87. *The New Yorker*, Volume 45, Issues 41-45, 1969, p. 27.
88. Turse, Nick (2008). "A My Lai a Month". *The Nation.*
89. Nelson, Deborah (2008-11-03). *The War Behind Me: Vietnam Veterans Confront the Truth about U.S.* York: Basic Books. ISBN 0-465-00527-6.
90. Linder, Douglas (1999). "Biographies of Key Figures in the My Lai Courts-Martial: Oran Henderson". Law. Retrieved 2011-06-18.
91. McCarty, Mary. 45 years later, impact from My Lai case is still felt (http://www.stripes.com/news/vete-impact-from-my-lai-case-is-still-felt-1.212088). Dayton Daily News, March 16, 2013.

92. Neier, Aryeh. *War Crimes: Brutality, Genocide, Terror, and the Struggle for Justice.* New York: Times
93. Linder, Douglas (1999). "An Introduction to the My Lai Courts-Martial". Law.umkc.edu. Retrieved 20
94. Hersh, Seymour M. *Cover-Up: The Army's Secret Investigation of the Massacre at My Lai 4.* New York 1972.
95. Marshall, Burke; Goldstein, Joseph (April 2, 1976). "Learning From My Lai: A Proposal on War Crime. *Times*. p. 26.
96. Taylor, Telford. *Nuremberg and Vietnam: An American Tragedy.* Chicago: Quadrangle Books, 1970, Oliver, Kendrick. *The My Lai Massacre in American History and Memory.* Manchester: Manchester U 2006, p. 112.
97. Teitel, Martin (1972-06-06). "Again, the Suffering of Mylai". *New York Times*. p. 45. Retrieved 2008-0
98. Esper, George. 'It's Something You've Got to Live With': My Lai Memories Haunt Soldiers. (http://artic 988-03-13/news/mn-1573_1 front-lines) Los Angeles Times, March 13, 1988.
99. Complete Program Transcript . My Lai. WGBH American Experience | PBS (http://www.pbs.org/wgb nce/features/transcript/mylai-transcript/)
100. 'Blood and fire' of My Lai remembered 30 years later. (http://www.cnn.com/WORLD/9803/16/my.lai/) 1998
101. My Lai Survivors Gather to Pray for Victims, Peace 40 Years After Massacre. (http://www.foxnews.co6/my-lai-survivors-gather-to-pray-for-victims-peace-40-years-after-massacre/)Associated Press, Marc

102. Siegel, R. "My Lai Officer Apologizes for Massacre" (http://www.npr.org/templates/story/story.php?st&ps-cprs) All Things Considered, NPR, Aug 21, 2009
103. Calley Apologizes for 1968 My Lai Massacre (http://www.democracynow.org/2009/8/24/calley_apolo y_lai). A video report by *Democracy Now!*
104. "Ex-Vietnam lieutenant apologizes for massacre". *The Seattle Times.* August 21, 2009. Archived from

Welcome to Domico Investments, You are welcome to our company, Our Company is 50 years old, we have more businesses for sale then any other business broker in the Delaware Valley.

The hottest businesses that you can list right now are Laundromats and Bagel Shops, we have over 100 Non Circumvention Agreements sign by buyers for those two businesses. If you spend one hour a day listing those two items you will easily make one hundred k next year. We have over 80 pizza places for sale, but the last one we sold was 4 months ago that's a long time for us. Now Sal Mininino, our top listing agent has 30 listed, he has agreed to pay the selling sales person ⅓ of the commission if they sale any of them, I will send a list to everyone.

I started selling Motels back in the 70s when most of the Indian people came over here they were mostly Engineers, They would buy a motel and move in, so they had a place to live . the wife's would work in the datetime and the husband would work at night, Originally the Italian people owned them all and they always paid a 10 percent commission, But not the sellers are paying only 5 percent, but that's still a lot of money, I sold one 2 weeks ago. We do lots of large syndications County Clubs, Marinas Wineries, Driving Ranges, River Rafting Companies, Etc. These are good Limited Partnerships to get involved with, I have done at leased 18 large deals like that over the years mostly Large Restaurant deals. Some of the ones I've done where Lucian's Old Tavern, now Lucien's Manor in Berlin, Executive Banquets in Vineland, How the Ramada Inn, Louisiana Seafood House in Alexandria Virginia, Domico's Seafood House in North Beach Maryland also a chain of Delis, Joe's Diner in Westville now Gate Way Diner, to many to mention. I wrote three books on Real Estate, not the ones you learn to flap houses with ,but Commercial Industrial ones, where you bay a shopping Center, convert it to condominiums and the sell the spaces to the tenants that are now renting them. I converted many apartment complexes to Condominiums and many motels into condominium rooms and sold them out. Also a couple Marinas converting them into condo slips. And selling them for $1000 a foot of the boa, 30 foot boat $30,000 Etc., You can actually do whatever you want when you work for us. We are only interested in receiving the commissions on the deals . If you want to do a deal yourself I can always guild you though the process., for example if you were buy a warehouse with a 6 dollar a year per sq. foot income ,and you wanted to put little cages in side 10 by 10,10 by 20 like self-storage and increase the income from 6 dollars sq. ft a year to 25.00 a sq ft a year, you could do that. I put a syndication together We formed a limited partnership, and took the place over and made a 250 seat restaurant out of it. We will always work with our people to make them very successful. You can make large commissions and put the money back in deals. You are working for a very good company that will help you make your first million. The Market for pizza places which we have many for sale, is dropping off.

Spend an hour a day on the phone getting listings, big demand for Bagel Shops and Laundromats right now. Pick up my first book. "How to make a million dollars a year in Real Estate and make it happen. documents. The letters describe common occurrences of civilian killings during population pacific Army policy also stressed very high body counts and this resulted in dead civilians being marked d combatants. Alluding to indiscriminate killings described as unavoidable, the commander of the 9t in Major General Julian Ewell, in September 1969, submitted a confidential report to Westmoreland a generals describing the countryside in some areas of Vietnam as resembling the battlefields of Ver

In July 1969, the Office of Provost Marshal General of the Army began to examine the evidence co
General Peers inquiry regarding possible criminal charges. Eventually, Calley was charged with se premeditated murder in September 1969, and 25 other officers and enlisted men were later charged crimes.

Courts Martial

On November 17, 1970, a court-martial in the United States charged 14 officers, including Major (Koster, the Americal Division's commanding officer, with suppressing information related to the ir the charges were later dropped. Brigade commander Colonel Henderson was the only high ranking officer who stood trial on charges relating to the cover-up of the My Lai massacre; he was acquitte 17, 1971.[90]

During the four-month-long trial, Lieutenant Calley consistently claimed that he was following ord commanding officer, Captain Medina. Despite that, he was convicted and sentenced to life in prison 1971, after being found guilty of premeditated murder of not fewer than twenty people. Two days I Richard Nixon made the controversial decision to have Calley released from armed custody at Fort Georgia, and put under house arrest pending appeal of his sentence. Calley's conviction was upheld Court of Military Review in 1973 and by the U.S. Court of Military Appeals in 1974. [91] In Augus sentence was reduced by the Convening Authority from life to twenty years. Calley would eventua and one-half years under house arrest at Fort Benning including three months in a disciplinary barr Leavenworth, Kansas. In September 1974, he was paroled by the Secretary of the Army Howard C

In a separate trial, Captain Medina denied giving the orders that led to the massacre, and was acqui charges, effectively negating the prosecution's theory of "command responsibility", now referred to standard". Several months after his acquittal, however, Medina admitted that he had suppressed ev lied to Colonel Henderson about the number of civilian deaths.[93] Captain Kotouc, an intelligence 11th Brigade, was also court-martialed and found not guilty. Major General Koster was demoted tc general and lost his position as the Superintendent of West Point. His deputy, Brigadier General Yc letter of censure. Both were stripped of Distinguished Service Medals which had been awarded for Vietnam.[94]

Most of the enlisted men who were involved in the events at My Lai had already left military service the 26 men initially charged, Lieutenant Calley was the only one convicted.

Some have argued that the outcome of the Mỹ Lai courts-martial failed to uphold the laws of war

A Vietnamese Girl Unveils Everything About Her Culture

Andy: How common is it to be intimate with your boyfriend before marriage?

Phuong: It used to be **very** strict. But now, especially young people, they are more open minded about it. Today, I am guessing over 70% of couples have sex before marriage. Their issue is finding privacy since they can't go to their parent's house. Sometimes they find a hotel room.

Of course, the parents don't usually support this.

Andy: Why would : Vietnamese girl prefer to date foreign men?

Phuong: it's an interesting question haha! Of course no Vietnamese girl is the same, but I think there are some reasons. I will try to clarity them below.

- **Appearance:** In general, Western men look very manly. Big, tall and great body. And I think all women want to feel safe and protected by their man.
- **Finances:** Some, but not all, Vietnamese girls believe that all Western men are rich. But I think many girls have been disappointed, because not all are rich. Some of them even have issues surviving here in Saigon!
- **Immigration:** Yes it's true. Many girls are dreaming of living in a Western country! Some will choose a man just to be able to move to his country.
- **Respect:** A girl may feel she gets more respect from a Western man. Many Vietnamese men are very violent and may hit their women. They can also be lazy, drink a lot and have no goals in life. Don't get me wrong, there are many good Vietnamese men, but many have been badly influenced from our culture and parents. In the West everyone is equal.
- **Love:** With that being said, I still believe the most important reason is love. That is what keeps a relationship together.

Andy: How does the Vietnamese society view a local girl dating a foreign man? How does her family react to this? They generally accepting of it?

Phuong: Well, today it's very common to see a local Vietnamese girl dating a Western man. You even see couples with big age differences. I think most parents won't have any issues with their daughter dating a Western man. I think the ones that don't support it are concerned about language and religion, or that their daughter will move to another country. But family has no issues with this.

Andy: Is the typical Vietnamese girl open move with her husband to another country?

Phuong: In Vietnamese culture, we say that after the marriage, Wherever the man is, it's the girl's home. Normally she will accept to move to another country. However, the man also need to consider many things, including the girl's family situation.

Andy: Are there things a Westerner need to know when visiting his Vietnamese girlfriend's family?

Phuong: Yup! Of course! I think you need to know some basic customs, otherwise you will be viewed as impolite haha. For example, if they invite you for dinner, it's customary to let the eldest family member pick up the chopstick and start eating first. It shows respect. Also, during the meal, feel free to serve food to other people. This shows you are caring and Vietnamese really like this. Also, when you greet a senior family member, you should bow.

To bow is one of the first things we teach our children!

Religion

Andy: How big of a part does religion play in Vietnamese daily life?

Phuong: in Vietnam, 50% of people are Buddhists, 30% are Catholics and 20% have other religions. Religion plays a significant part in our life. For example, I am a Buddhist and I have been going to temples ever since I was a child. Sometimes my religion gives me guidance when I need to make decisions.

Andy: Are there any issues if the boyfriend is from another religion?

Phuong: If the family are Buddhists, I say no. But I am not sure about the other religions. I had one Christian friend that married a Buddhist man, and he had to change his religion because of pressure from her parents. My parents would never do this.

Andy: I have heard many stories that the Vietnamese are a bit superstitious and believe in Ghosts. Tell us a little about that.

Phuong: Haha yes! Since I was a child, I have heard many ghost stories from my grandparents.
Sometimes you will see Vietnamese people burning items on the street like fake money. clothes, jewelry, etc. They might also spread rice, salt, wine, candies, cake, etc. We believe when the evil spirit receive it, they will bring us luck. If not, they will interfere with our life or business. But once you start doing this, you can't stop, because the evil spirits will remind you in some bad way haha.

Closing Thoughts With a Vietnamese Girl

Andy: Well, we have now reached the end of our interview, and I want to wrap it up with final questions.

What is the best thing about living in Vietnam? Worst thing? What would you like to change about your country?

Phuong: Well, starting with the best things first, I think Vietnam has cheaper cost of living compared with other countries. Also, life is less stressful because people don't work like crazy. We always fed time to spend with our families and friends. Finally, Vietnamese people are very friendly, you will have no problem getting along with most people here.

Regarding the worst things, I would say safety. There are many thieves and robbers on our streets. And then we have crazy traffic and bad air pollution.

If there is one thing I'd like to change about my country, it would be selfishness. I believe this is the number one reason my country is improving too slowly. For example, we need to throw the garbage into trash cans and not on the street. We also should not cut in line, etc . . .

Andy: And last questions are—what do you think is the worst quality in a Vietnamese girl? What I the best?

Phuong: think the worst quality their dependence on other people. It's not only for financial support but also can be a variety of things. They are also bound by many ancient rules they believe are correct.

Their best quality is that they are very faithful and have a strong dedication to family. Our concept of family is very valuable and sacred, so we won't give up on the relationship so easy!

PS: Make sure to check out ***Andy's website***, You can meet Vietnamese girls ***here***.

75. "Interview on CNN's Larry King Live with Secretary Colin L. Powell". May 4, 2004. Archived from 2006-03-09. Retrieved March 16, 2006.
76. "Text of Ron Ridenhour's 1969 letter". Law.umkc.edu. 1969-03-29. Retrieved 2012-07-21.
77. "The Heroes of My Lai". Law.umkc.edu. December 1994. Retrieved 2012-07-21.
78. The Men Talked of the Killing (https://news.google.com/newspapers?id=FEUyAAAAIBAJ&sjid=2bU=979,32153&dq=michael+terry+my+lai&hl=en). *The Palm Beach Post*, June 1, 1970.
79. The Heroes of My Lai: Ron Ridenhour's Story (http://law2.umkc.edu/faculty/projects/frials/mylai/MyN) Ridenhour's own account during the conference on My Lai at Tulane University in New Orleans, L December 1994.
80. "Mo Udall, The Education of a Congressman". Udall.gov. Retrieved 2011-06-18.
81. Brooke, Edward William (2007). *Bridging the Divide: My Life*. Rutgers University Press. 166. ISBN
82. Friday, Dec. 05, 1969 (1969-12-05). "The Press: Miscue on the Massacre". Time.com. Retrieved 2011-
83. Oliver, Kendrick (2006). *The My Lai Massacre in American History and Memory*. Manchester: Manch Press. p. 48. ISBN 0719068916.
84. Linder, Douglas (1999). "Biography of General William R. Peers". Law.umkc.edu. Retrieved 2011-06-
85. "Lte Frank Akeley Barker". Thewall-usa.com. 1967-11-26. Retrieved 2011-06-18.
86. Schell, Jonathan. *The Military Half: An Account of Destruction in Quang Ngai and Quang Tin*. New York

87. *The New Yorker*, Volume 45, Issues 41-45, 1969, p. 27.
88. Turse, Nick (2008). "A My Lai a Month". *The Nation*.
89. Nelson, Deborah (2008-11-03). *The War Behind Me: Vietnam Veterans Confront the Truth about U.S.* York: Basic Books. ISBN 0-465-00527-6.
90. Linder, Douglas (1999). "Biographies of Key Figures in the My Lai Courts-Martial: Oran Henderson". Law. Retrieved 2011-06-18.
91. McCarty, Mary. 45 years later, impact from My Lai case is still felt (http://www.stripes.com/news/vete-impact-from-my-lai-case-is-still-felt-1.212088). Dayton Daily News, March 16, 2013.
92. Neier, Aryeh. *War Crimes: Brutality, Genocide, Terror, and the Struggle for Justice.* New York: Times
93. Linder, Douglas (1999). "An Introduction to the My Lai Courts-Martial". Law.umkc.edu. Retrieved 20
94. Hersh, Seymour M. *Cover-Up: The Army's Secret Investigation of the Massacre at My Lai 4.* New York 1972.
95. Marshall, Burke; Goldstein, Joseph (April 2, 1976). "Learning From My Lai: A Proposal on War Crim *Times*. p. 26.
96. Taylor, Telford. *Nuremberg and Vietnam: An American Tragedy.* Chicago: Quadrangle Books, 1970, Oliver, Kendrick. *The My Lai Massacre in American History and Memory.* Manchester: Manchester U 2006, p. 112.
97. Teitel, Martin (1972-06-06). "Again, the Suffering of Mylai". *New York Times.* p. 45. Retrieved 2008-0
98. Esper, George. It's Something You've Got to Live With': My Lai Memories Haunt Soldiers. (http://artic 988-03-13/

news/mn-1573_1_front-lines) Los Angeles Times, March 13, 1988.
99. Complete Program Transcript. My Lai. WGBH American Experience | PBS (http://www.pbs.org/wgb nce/features/transcript/mylai-transcript/)
100. 'Blood and fire' of My Lai remembered 30 years later. (http://www.cnn.com/WORLD/9803/16/my.lai/) 1998
101. My Lai Survivors Gather to Pray for Victims, Peace 40 Years After Massacre. (http://www.foxnews.com6/my-lai-survivors-gather-to-pray-for-victims-peace-40-years-after-massacre/) *Associated Press,* Marc
102. Siegel, R. "My Lai Officer Apologizes for Massacre" (http://www.npr.org/templates/story/story.php?st&ps-cprs) *All Things Considered*, NPR, Aug 21, 2009
103. Calley Apologizes for 1968 My Lai Massacre (http://www.democracynow.org/2009/8/24/calley_apolo y_ lai). A video report by *Democracy Now!*
104. "Ex—Vietnam lieutenant apologizes for massacre". The Seattle Times. August 21, 2009. Archived from
109. La Croix, Lawrence C. Reflection on My Lai. (http://articles.latimes.com/1993-03-25/local/me-14700 er-lai-operation-pinkville) *Los Angeles Times*, March 25, 1993
110. Search for "Brooks" (http://thewall-usa.com/search.asp) Names on the Wall, The Vietnam Veterans Me
111. Calley admits slayings on Capt. Medina's order. (https://news.google.com/newspapers?id=NxYuAAA/MDAAAAIBAJ&pg=1493,6642255&dq=my+lai&hl=en) Rome News-Tribune, February 23, 1971.
112. General Heard My Lai Radio Conversations: Pentagon Says Americal Commander Was in Copter During

Massacre http://pgasb.pqarchiver.com/latimes/doc/156398291.html?FM-ABS&FMTS=ABS:Al&ty.=Dec%2019,%201969&author-&pub=Los%20Angeles%20Times&edition=&startpage=&desc=GeneMy%20Lai%20Radio%20Conversations). *Los Angeles Times,* December 19, 1969.

113. Calley jury to call own witnesses. (https://news.google.com/newspapers?id=xd8jAAAAIBAJ&sjid-fCg-6570,2098116&dq=my+lai&hl=en) *The Milwaukee Journal,* March 6, 1971.

114. "Peers Report: Captain Ernset Medina". Law.umke.edu. Retrieved 2011-06-18.

115. Henderson Witness Admits False Statement about My Lai (https://news.google.com/ewspapers?id=G&sjid=Q8kEAAAAIBAJ&pg=5046,4600204&dq=my+lai+medina&hl=en). *Daytona Beach Morning.* September 17, 1971.

116. Hersh, Seymour M. *Cover-Up: the Army's Secret Investigation of the Massacre at My Lai 4.* New York 1972.

117. Peers, William R. *The My Lai Inquiry.* New York: Norton, 1979.

118. Lelyveld, Joseph. A soldier who refused to fire at Songmy.(http://select.nytimes.com/gst/abstract.html45F127A93C6A81789D95F4D8685F9) *The New York Times,* December 14, 1969.

119. *The My Lai Massacre in American History and Memory.* Manchester University Press. 2006. ISBN 97:Retrieved 2011-06-18.

120. "The Ethical Humanist Award: New York Society for Ethical Culture". Nysec.org. Retrieved 2011-06-:
121. Timeline: Charlie Company and the Massacre at My Lai. (http://www.pbs.org/wgbh/americanexperien c/mylai-massacre/)PBS, American Experience.
122. Lawrence C. La Croix. Reflection on My Lai (http://articles.latimes.com/1993-03-25/local/me-14700_ er-lai-operation-pinkville). *Los Angeles Time,* March 25, 1993.
123. In Cally testimony: Soldier refused "order". (https://news.google.com/newspapers?id=WppaAAAAIB/AAIBAJ&pg=5797,4629881&dq-james+joseph+dursi&hl=en) *Ellensburg Daily Record,* December 7,
124. Digital History. (http://www.digitalhistory.uh.edu/learning_history/vietnam/vietnam_mylai.cfm) Archi chive.org/web/20131007064903/http://www.digitalhistory.uh.edu/learning_history/vietnam/vietnam_n7, 2013, at the Wayback Machine. An online textbook maintained by the University of Utah.
125. "Armed Forces: The My Lai Trials Begin". *Time.* November 2, 1970. Retrieved May 2, 2010.
126. War Hero Relives Day He Refused To Murder. (http://articles.orlandosentinel.com/1989-11-19/news/8: ley-lai-4-calley) *Orlando Sentinel,* November 19, 1989.

127. Allison, William Thomas. My Lai: An American Atrocity in the Vietnam War.(https://books.google.480E9vxIC&printsec=frontcover&dq=My+Lai:+An+American+Atrocity+in+the+Vietnam+War&hl=e rUpPSFbK14AOwsoDQCA&ved=0CCEQ6AEwAA#v=onepage&q=My%20Lai%3A%20An%20Amy%20in%20the%20Vietnam%20War&f=false) Baltimore: Johns Hopkins University Press, 2012.
128. "Remember My Lai (http://www.pbs.org/wgbh/pages/frontline/programs/transcripts/714.html)".WGB Foundation, May 23, 1989. Retrieved on June 28, 2009.
129. *History of the 1st Battalion 20th Infantry* (http://www.1-20infantry.org/rvnhist.htm)A History Of The Formation At Schofield Barracks, Hawaii Through Its Deactivation After Service In The Republic Of Research And Compilation By Cpt. Chuck Seketa.
130. Charlie Company (http://www.charlie1-20.org/) A website with history of the Charlie Company
131. Timeline: Charlie Company and the Massacre at My Lai (http://www.pbs.org/wgbh/americanexperience/mylai-massacre/)
132. "1st Battalion, 20th Infantry Regiment, HHQ Company Roster 1968". Retrieved 11 March 2016.

www.ingramcontent.com/pod-product-compliance
Lightning Source LLC
LaVergne TN
LVHW052004060526
838201LV00059B/3833